TO:

FROM:

THE
SIMPLE TRUTHS
OF SERVICE

INSPIRED BY JOHNNY THE BAGGER®

KEN BLANCHARD
AND BARBARA A. GLANZ

Small books. **BIG IMPACT.**

IGNITE READS
spark impact in just one hour

Photo Credits
Cover: freepik.com
Internals: freepik.com; page vi, Fraser Cottrell/Unsplash; page viii-ix, TJ Kolesnik/Unsplash; page x, Corey Hodgson/Unsplash; page xiv, PointImages/GettyImages; page 2, Annie Spratt/Unsplash; page 6, Robert Kneschke/Shutterstock; page 9, solidcolours/GettyImages; page 10-11, gopixa/GettyImages; page 12-13, ronstik/GettyImages; page 14, Juanmonino/iStock; page 18, Hanny Naibaho/Unsplash; page 21, Barn Images/Unsplash; page 22-23, Crew/Unsplash; page 26, Igor Ovsyannykov/Unsplash; page 28, Valentin Antonucci/Unsplash; page 31, Jenpol/GettyImages; page 34, Zac Ong/Unsplash; page 37, artisteer/GettyImages; page 39, moose henderson/GettyImages; page, 42-43 Hero Images/GettyImages; page 46, CHAIWATPHOTOS/GettyImages; page 49, Gho Rhy Yan/Unsplash; page 50-51, Simon Matzinger/Unsplash; page 54, noipornpan/GettyImages; page 60, epicurean/iStock; page 63, welcomia/GettyImages; page 66-67, Evan Kirby/Unsplash; page 70, DragonImages/GettyImages; page 76, solidcolours/iStock; page 78, PeopleImages/iStock; page 81, Jon Tyson/Unsplash; page 82-83, jacoblund/GettyImages; page 86, VictorHuang/GettyImages; page 89, shutter_m/GettyImages; page 92, Jessica Ruscello/Unsplash; page 94, Ian Pham/Unsplash; page 96, blackred/iStock; page 99, Fascinadora/GettyImages; page 100, kirin_photo/iStock; page 103, monkeybusinessimages/GettyImages; page 104, KucherAV/GettyImages

Published by Simple Truths, an imprint of Sourcebooks, Inc.
P.O. Box 4410, Naperville, Illinois 60567-4410
(630) 961-3900
Fax: (630) 961-2168
sourcebooks.com

Printed and bound in China.
OGP 10 9 8 7 6 5 4 3 2

CONTENTS

INTRODUCTION

By Ken Blanchard

Years ago, you could abuse customers and they had no choice but to go along with it. There was nobody else doing your business. Today, things are very different. If you don't take care of your customers, somebody else is waiting, ready, and willing to do it.

Today, your competitive advantage is not the quality of your product or service. If you don't have a high-quality product or service, you're not even in the game. Your competitive edge today cannot be your price, because someone can always undercut your price. What you need is a fair price. The real competitive edge

you have today is how you treat your customers. The one thing your competition can't take away from you is the relationship your people have with your customers.

That's why I fell in love with Barbara Glanz's story of Johnny the Bagger. With her blessing, I've shared the story of Johnny the Bagger over and over again, everywhere I go, to illustrate that every person can make a difference for their customers.

Let me give you an example of the impact this story has had. Our training and consulting company was asked to develop a customer service training program for all the frontline employees involved in the opening of the new San Diego Padres stadium, Petco Park. Since the building of the park had been a controversial proposition, the top managers wanted the fans to have a very special experience in the new park. As we helped them set the customer service vision for the park, they decided they were in the Major League memory business. Every night, every employee—whether in food service, maintenance, security, or what have you—was

expected to focus their energy on creating good fan memories.

As part of the training, I made a short video, telling the story of Johnny. I ended the video looking into the camera and saying directly to every park employee, *"Are you going to be a Johnny tonight?"* This video was

shown to everyone, no matter whether they were part-time or full-time.

A number of the department managers told me that every night before the gates opened, they would ask their people, "Are you going to be a Johnny tonight?" The first summer Petco Park was in business, they got

7,500 unsolicited notes and letters from fans telling stories of how they had been blown away by the service they had received from someone in the park.

For example, a customer ordered two fish tacos at one of the concession stands. When he got back to his seat, he took a bite and discovered they had given him chicken tacos. Since he was yearning for fish tacos, he returned to the concession stand to exchange them. When he told the counter person what had happened, the young man's initial response was, "Let me talk to my supervisor." A more experienced worker next to him heard the conversation and said, "You don't have to ask the supervisor. This man did not get what he wanted, so give him two fish tacos. We work for him."

Another sports fan brought her baby to the game one night and ran out of milk. She went to one of the concession stands and asked for some milk. A young man behind the counter said, "We don't sell milk here, but I know where I can get it. What's your seat number?" This young man got someone to cover his station while he raced out of the ballpark and down the street to a 7-Eleven, where he bought some milk. He came back, heated the milk up, and took it to the waiting mother. She couldn't believe it.

Neither will you after you read the Johnny story and see how you and everyone in your organization can make a difference in your customers' lives. The memories you create will keep people coming back—and bringing their friends—for years to come.

"

The one thing your competition can't take away from you is the relationship your people have with your customers.

—Ken Blanchard

"

JOHNNY THE BAGGER

By Barbara Glanz

As an author and professional speaker, I travel all over the world and speak to groups about one of my favorite topics: building customer loyalty. A few years ago, I was leading a customer service session for a large supermarket chain, where I had the opportunity to speak to a crowd of three thousand frontline service people—truck drivers, cashiers, baggers, produce people, stockers, floral specialists, bakers, and others.

During the course of my presentation, I said, "Every one of you can make a difference and create meaningful memories for your customers that will motivate them to come back. How?"

PUT YOUR
PERSONAL SIGNATURE
ON THE JOB.

"Go home tonight and think about something you can do for your customers to make them feel special—a memory that will make them want to come back and shop at your store again."

I then directed the audience's attention to one of my personal signatures: the nearly one hundred bright-colored, handmade posters lining the walls, printed with all kinds of quotations.

Whether I'm speaking to thirty or three thousand people, I always line the walls of the room or ballroom with these posters, because they change the feeling in the room by adding color, inspiration, and fun. They take a lot of extra time to put up, and they're bulky to lug around the country, but they make me stand out as a speaker and provide a wonderful memory for audiences, so they are well worth the extra effort.

There are lots of ways you can give your own personal signature to your work. For example, I know a baggage attendant who decided his personal signature would be to collect all the luggage tags that fell off customers' suitcases. In the past, the tags had been simply tossed into the garbage. The attendant decided that in his free time he would send the tags back to their owners with a note that read,

"THANK YOU FOR FLYING WITH US."

3

I met a graphic artist who always encloses a piece of sugarless gum in everything he sends his customers so they never throw away anything from him. I heard of a senior manager who uses stickers and tissues as his personal signature. When the news is something he knows they won't like very much, he staples a piece of Kleenex to the corner of the memo.

BUT WHENEVER HE SENDS A MEMO WITH GOOD NEWS, HE ATTACHES A SMILEY FACE STICKER.

I always leave my telephone number and email address with audiences, encouraging them to call me if they have questions or want to share a

success story they experience by adding a personal signature to their work. About a month after I had spoken to the supermarket folks, I received a call from a frontline customer contact person, a nineteen-year-old bagger named Johnny.

The caller, who proudly informed me that he was a young man with Down syndrome, told me his story.

"Barbara, I liked what you talked about!" Johnny said excitedly. "But I didn't think I could do anything special for our customers. After all, I'm just a bagger. Then I had an idea."

Johnny had decided that every night when he came home from work, he would find a thought for the day.

"If I can't find a saying I like," Johnny said proudly, "I think one up!"

When Johnny had a good saying, his dad helped him enter his "Thought for the Day" six times on a page in the computer. Every night they printed out fifty pages. Johnny cut out each quote and signed his name on the back of every one of them.

"Then I put them in a paper bag I keep beside me at work," he continued. "When I finish bagging someone's groceries, I put my Thought for the Day in their bag and say, 'Thanks for shopping with us.'"

It touched me to think that this young man—with a job that most people would say is not important—had made it important by creating precious memories for all his customers.

A month later, the store manager called me. He said, "Barbara, you won't believe what happened today. When I was making my rounds and got up front where the cashiers are, I found the line at Johnny's checkout was three times longer than anyone else's! It went all the way down the frozen food aisle. I was concerned, so I announced, 'Get more cashiers out here; get more lanes open!' all the while trying to get people to change lanes. But no one would move. They all said, 'No, it's okay. We want to be in Johnny's lane. We want his Thought for the Day.'"

The store manager continued, "It was a joy to watch

7

Johnny delight the customers. I got a lump in my throat when one woman came up and grabbed my hand and said, 'I used to shop at your store only once a week, but now I come in every time I go by, because I want to get Johnny's Thought for the Day.'"

"I imagine that helps the bottom line," I said to the manager. He replied,

"YOU BET!

WHO DO YOU THINK IS THE MOST IMPORTANT PERSON IN OUR WHOLE STORE NOW?

JOHNNY, OF COURSE!"

A few months later, the store manager called me again. "Barbara," he said, "Johnny has transformed our store. Now, when the floral department has a broken

flower or an unused corsage, they go out on the floor and find an elderly woman or a little girl and pin it on them.

"One of our butchers loves Snoopy. He bought thousands of Snoopy stickers and each time he wraps a piece of meat, he puts a sticker on it. All of our cashiers now have their own personal signature. Everyone's having a lot of fun creating memories.

"OUR CUSTOMERS ARE
TALKING ABOUT US...IN A
GOOD WAY, COMING BACK,
AND BRINGING THEIR
FRIENDS."

What a wonderful spirit of service spread throughout that store—and all because of one young man with Down syndrome who decided he could make a difference! As I tell my audiences, *"Every one of us in this room can make a difference. We can all be a Johnny."*

And with tears in nearly every eye, they agree.

"It is not how much we do, but how much love we put in the doing."

—Mother Teresa

THE SIMPLE TRUTHS OF GREAT SERVICE

By Ken Blanchard

The following stories of great service are simple but powerful. They're all about creating memories, building relationships, using your unique gifts, and caring for people. No matter what your job or position is in an organization, the real question is:

ARE YOU GOING TO CHOOSE TO BE A JOHNNY TODAY?

1
GREAT SERVICE
INSPIRES STORIES

1

A number of years ago, Sheldon Bowles and I wrote a book called *Raving Fans.* We argued that to keep your customers today, you can't be content just to satisfy them; you have to create "raving fans." These are customers who are so excited about the way you treat them that they want to tell stories about you; they become part of your sales force. That's exactly what Johnny did—he created raving fan customers.

My mother, when she was ninety, gave me a beautiful example of raving fan service. One day, she went to her refrigerator to get some ice. When she opened the ice section, water came pouring out; something clearly was wrong. Since she was an independent cuss and wanted to solve the problem without bothering me, she called appliance service companies one after the other, only to be told that the earliest anyone could visit her was in three weeks.

Now, when you are ninety years old, three weeks is a long time. Discouraged, she was about to call me for help when she saw a little ad that read, "Sameday service." She called the number, and soon a friendly voice was saying, "We'd be happy to fix your refrigerator today, Mrs. Blanchard. When would you like us to come?"

"I have a choice?" my mom responded in amazement.

"Absolutely," the friendly voice said.

"How about two o'clock?" Mom replied.

Not only did a serviceman show up at two, he even had tools and knew what a refrigerator was. He fixed the fridge, and as he was leaving, he handed his business card to my amazed and happy mom. It had his home phone number on the back. "Anytime, night or day, you have a problem with this refrigerator, you can give me a call," he said.

What do you think my mother was doing for the next three days? She was calling everyone she knew who was still alive about the service she had received. She had become a raving fan. That's exactly how the customers in Johnny's store felt about him.

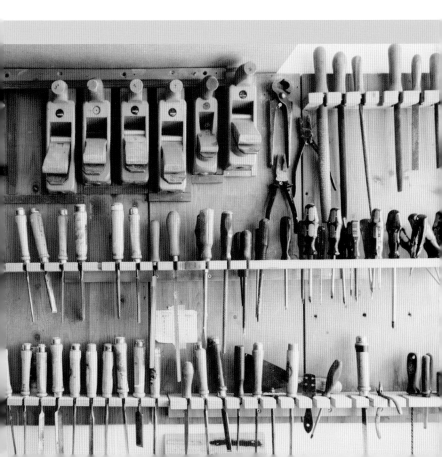

"Aim for service, and success will follow."

—Albert Schweitzer

2
GREAT SERVICE USES OUTSIDE-THE-BOX THINKING

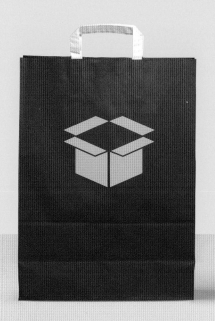

2

One way to get customers to brag about you is to begin thinking outside the box. That's exactly what the owner of the appliance repair company my mother bragged about did. When I called him to find out how he could service people the day they called, he explained his story. It turned out that he had been a fix-it man in Massachusetts. Because of his health, his doctors suggested he move to a warmer climate. When he got to San Diego, he would find out when people were moving into a house they had just bought. He would knock on the door and tell them he was a fix-it man, and if they needed any painting or repairs done, he would be happy to do it at a reasonable price.

All he asked was that they agree to refer him to other customers if they liked his work.

This guy always showed up on time, did what he said he would do with high quality, and charged a reasonable price. People loved his work. He built his business up so much that when old customers would call to get him to do something, very often he didn't have time because he was so busy. A number of people suggested to him that he start his own company. But he was reluctant, because he was concerned about managing employees and having a big payroll.

One night, he woke up with a brilliant idea. About 30 percent of the people living in San Diego are retirees. Many retirees are bored. They'd love to have something to do, and if they could help other people, that'd be even more special. So he put an ad in the local paper that read:

**RETIREES:
IF YOU'RE GOOD
AT FIXING THINGS
AND WANT TO HELP
PEOPLE AND MAKE
SOME EXTRA MONEY,
GIVE ME A CALL.**

He ended up with twenty-five to thirty retirees on call every single day. So if a customer like my mother called, he had someone he could send out to her. And he didn't have the problem of a big payroll. If the people didn't work, they didn't get paid. Laughingly, he told me that he had a hard time paying some of the people because it goofed up their Social Security. They just loved the work.

How's that for out-of-the-box thinking?
Johnny didn't do too badly on that score, either.

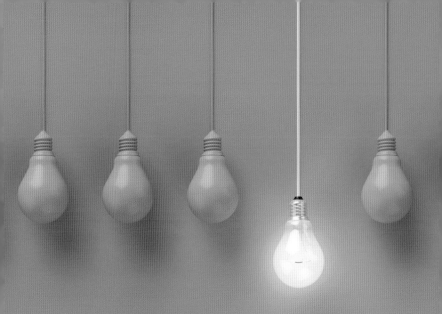

"The best way to have
a good idea is to have
lots of ideas."

—Linus Pauling

3
GREAT SERVICE
IS A CHOICE

3

No one can make you serve customers well. That's because great service is a choice. Years ago, my friend Harvey Mackay told me a wonderful story about a cab driver that proved this point.

Harvey was waiting in line for a ride at the airport. When a cab pulled up, the first thing Harvey noticed was that the taxi was polished to a bright shine. Smartly dressed in a white shirt, black tie, and freshly pressed black slacks, the cab driver jumped out and rounded the car to open the back passenger door for Harvey. He handed my friend a laminated card and said, "I'm Wally, your driver. While I'm loading your bags in the trunk, I'd like you to read my mission statement."

Taken aback, Harvey read the card.

Wally's Mission Statement:

To get my customers to their destination in the quickest, safest, and cheapest way possible in a friendly environment.

This blew Harvey away. Especially when he noticed that the inside of the cab matched the outside—spotlessly clean!

As he slid behind the wheel, Wally said, "Would you like a cup of coffee? I have a thermos of regular and one of decaf."

My friend said jokingly, "No, I'd prefer a soft drink."

Wally smiled and said, "No problem. I have a cooler up front with regular and Diet Coke, water, and orange juice."

Almost stuttering, Harvey said, "I'll take a Diet Coke."

Handing him his drink, Wally said, "If you'd like something to read, I have the *Wall Street Journal*, *Time*, *Sports Illustrated,* and *USA Today.*"

As they were pulling away, Wally handed my friend another laminated card. "These are the stations I get and the music they play, if you'd like to listen to the radio."

And as if that weren't enough, Wally told Harvey that he had the air-conditioning on and asked if the temperature was comfortable for him. Then he advised Harvey

of the best route to his destination for that time of day. He also let him know that he'd be happy to chat and tell him about some of the sights or, if Harvey preferred, to leave him with his own thoughts.

"Tell me, Wally," my amazed friend asked the driver, "have you always served customers like this?"

Wally smiled into the rearview mirror. "No, not always. In fact, it's only been in the last two years. My first five years driving, I spent most of my time complaining like all the rest of the cabbies do. Then I heard the personal growth guru, Wayne Dyer, on the radio one day. He had just written a book called *You'll See It When You Believe It*. Dyer said if you get up in the morning expecting to have a bad day, you'll rarely disappoint yourself. He said, 'Stop complaining! Differentiate yourself from your competition. Don't be a duck. Be an eagle. Ducks quack and complain. Eagles soar above the crowd.'

"That hit me right between the eyes. Dyer was really talking about me. I was always quacking and

complaining, so I decided to change my attitude and become an eagle. I looked around at the other cabs and their drivers. The cabs were dirty, the drivers were unfriendly, and the customers were unhappy. So I decided to make some changes. I put in a few at a time. When my customers responded well, I did more."

"I take it this has paid off for you," Harvey said.

"It sure has," Wally replied. "My first year as an eagle, I doubled my income from the previous year. This year, I'll probably quadruple it. You were lucky to get me today. I don't sit at cabstands anymore. My customers call me for appointments on my cell phone or leave a message on my answering machine. If I can't pick them up myself, I get a reliable cabbie friend to do it, and I take a piece of the action."

Wally was phenomenal. He was running a limo ser- vice out of a taxi. I've probably told that story to more than fifty cab drivers over the years, and only two took the idea and ran with it. Whenever I go to their cities, I give them a call. The rest of the drivers quacked like ducks and told me all the reasons they couldn't do any of what I was suggesting.

Johnny the Bagger and Wally the Cab Driver made a different choice. They decided to stop quacking like ducks and start soaring like eagles. How about you?

"Always give people more than they expect to get."

—Nelson Boswell

4
GREAT SERVICE STARTS WITH A CLEAR VISION

4

Great service is not an accident. It starts with a clear vision around the kind of experience you want your customers to have.

In the early 1970s, when most gas stations were converting to self-service, my coauthor Sheldon Bowles said, "What a fabulous time to go to full service. There will be no competition." So he and his partners developed a full-service gas station called Domo Gas. They knew that if people had a choice, they certainly wouldn't choose to come to a gas station. They also knew that when customers did come, they wanted to get in and out as quickly as possible. The unique customer service vision Sheldon and his partners imagined was an Indianapolis 500 pit stop.

All the attendants at Domo Gas were dressed up in red jumpsuits. If you drove into a Domo gas station, two or three people would race out of the hut to your car. Somebody would look under the hood, somebody would clean the windows, and somebody would start pumping gas. As Sheldon and his partners rolled out this vision in more than 150 stations across western Canada, they killed the competition.

A gas station in northern California heard about this vision and went one step further. After serving a customer, they would hand that person a little brochure about their service that read: "P.S. We also sell gas."

Having a clear vision of great service is the key. Do you think Johnny the Bagger saw the vision Barbara painted?

"You see things;
and you say 'Why?'
But I dream things
that never were;
and I say 'Why not?'"

—George Bernard Shaw

5
GREAT SERVICE REQUIRES THAT EVERYONE CATCH THE VISION

5

I'll never forget the time I visited Give Kids The World Village in Orlando, Florida. If a kid is dying and has never been to Disneyland, SeaWorld, MGM, and the like, Give Kids The World provides that opportunity. Since 1986, they have brought more than 146,000 families to Orlando for a week at no cost to them.

The leadership of Give Kids The World decided that they were in the memory business. I was interested in how far down the organization that vision went. As I walked with the president one day, we passed a maintenance person cutting the grass. I went over to him and asked, "What business are you in here at Give Kids The World?"

He smiled and said, "We make memories."

I said, "How do you make memories? You just cut the grass."

He said, "I don't make memories by continuing to cut the grass when a family comes by. You can always tell who the sick kid is. So I stop what I'm doing and ask the sick kid or one of his brothers and sisters if they want to help me with my chores. We make memories."

Johnny the Bagger caught the vision Barbara had inspired. When Johnny put his quotations into a customer's bag, he was making wonderful memories for them and inspiring his associates to follow suit.

Cherish your vision and your dreams, as they are the children of your soul, the blueprints of your ultimate achievements.

—Napoleon Hill

6
GREAT SERVICE
SURPRISES PEOPLE

6

Over the years when I have experienced great service, I've often been caught off guard—even surprised.

I'll never forget a story Milt Garrett told me one day. Milt, who lived in Albuquerque, New Mexico, at the time, is a trainer and consultant who periodically has worked with our company. On a Friday night at the end of a week of training, he and his wife, Jane, took a walk. Jane said to him, "Milt, you missed my anniversary this week."

Surprised, Milt said, "What anniversary?"

"Five years cancer free," said Jane. Five years earlier, Jane had had a mastectomy. She and Milt had celebrated every year that she was cancer free.

Milt felt awful. He couldn't believe he had forgotten. The week before, he and Jane had talked about her needing a new car. Since their son was still in college in Australia, they'd decided to wait a year until he graduated. But that night, Milt said to himself, "Why am I waiting? I am so lucky Jane is still in my life."

The next morning, he called the Saturn dealership in Albuquerque and talked to one of their salespeople. I'm not kidding—the salesman's real name was Billy Graham. Milt explained the situation to Billy, saying that his kids had told him Jane really wanted a white car. "Could you get me a white Saturn by next Saturday, when I get back home from training?" Milt asked.

Billy told Milt that white Saturns were hard to get. "But if you're going to come in next Saturday, I'll have one ready," he said.

The next Saturday morning, Milt told Jane that he was running a bunch of errands, but he invited her to come with him so they could go out to lunch. During their drive, they passed the Saturn dealership. Milt told

Jane he had to stop in for some materials because he was giving a speech about Saturn to the Chamber of Commerce. When they entered the dealership, they saw only one car: a white Saturn in the center of the showroom.

"Milt, that's the kind of car I'd love to have!" Jane said. She ran over to the Saturn and, with a big grin on her face, got in. When she got out of the car and walked around the front of it, she let out a scream and began to cry. Milt had no idea what had happened. When he got to the front of the car, he saw a beautiful sign on the hood of the car that read:

Yes, Jane, this is your car!
Congratulations on five years cancer free.

Love,
Milt, Billy, and the whole Saturn staff

When Billy saw Milt and Jane coming, he had led everyone out of the showroom and into the parking lot, so that the couple could be alone. As they were crying in each other's arms, all of a sudden, they heard applause. They looked up to see everyone giving them a hand. It surprised and delighted them, to say the least.

What a wonderful way to create a special moment for your customers. In many ways, that's what Johnny the Bagger did—he surprised and delighted his customers.

"We do not remember days;
we remember moments."

—Cesare Pavese

7
GREAT SERVICE
BEGINS WITH
ANYONE

7

When it comes to great service, everyone makes a difference. For example, what's the most common wake-up call you get in a hotel today? The phone rings, but when you pick it up, there is no one there. The second most common wake-up call greets you with a recording. But again, no one is there. Today, if you pick up the phone on a wake-up call and there's a human being on the other end, you hardly know what to say.

While I was staying at the Marriott in Orlando, the phone rang for my seven o'clock wake-up call. I picked it up and a woman said, "Good morning, Dr. Blanchard. This is Teresa. It's seven o'clock. It's going to be seventy-five and beautiful in Orlando today, but your ticket says you're leaving. Where are you going?"

Taken aback, I stammered, "I'm going to New York City."

She countered with, "Let me look at the *USA Today* weather map. Oh no! It's going to be forty degrees and rainy in New York today. Can't you stay?"

Now where do you think I want to stay when I go to Orlando? I want to stay at the Marriott so I can talk to Teresa in the morning!

Take it from Johnny and Teresa—great service begins with anyone.

**Everybody can
be great because
everybody can serve.**

—Dr. Martin Luther King Jr.

8
GREAT SERVICE GOES THE EXTRA MILE

8

When people are allowed to go the extra mile for the customer, great service is the result.

Horst Schulze, one of the founders of the Ritz-Carlton Hotels, retired a few years ago as president and CEO. During Schulze's reign, after orientation and extensive training, every employee was given a $2,000 discretionary fund they could use to solve a customer problem without checking with anyone. They didn't even have to tell their boss. Schulze loved to collect stories about people really using this empowerment to make a difference.

One of my favorites is about a businessman who was staying at one of the Ritz-Carlton properties in

Atlanta. That day, he had to fly from Atlanta to Los Angeles and then from Los Angeles to Hawaii, because the next day at one o'clock, he was making a major speech to his international company. He was a little disorganized as he was leaving. On his way to the airport, he discovered he'd left behind his laptop computer, which contained all the PowerPoints he needed for his presentation. He tried to change his flights but couldn't. So he called the Ritz-Carlton and gave the operator his room number and the location of his computer in the room. He said, "Have housekeeping get it and overnight it to me. They have to guarantee delivery by ten o'clock tomorrow morning, because I need it for my one o'clock speech."

The next day, Schulze was wandering around the hotel, as he often did. When he got to housekeeping, he said, "Where's Mary today?"

Her coworkers said, "She's in Hawaii."

Schulze said, "Hawaii? What's she doing in Hawaii?"

He was told, "A guest left a computer in his room,

and he needs it for a speech today at one o'clock—and Mary doesn't trust overnight carrier services anymore." Now, you might think that Mary went for a vacation, but she came back on the next plane. And what do you think was waiting for her? A letter of commendation from Schulze and high fives around the hotel.

> **Johnny the Bagger was also allowed to use the power of his imagination in serving his customers. As a result of his going the extra mile, the entire store became energized, and it prospered.**

This reminds me of the wonderful short essay by Carl Holmes titled "And Then Some":

AND THEN SOME...these three little
words are the secret to success.
They are the difference between
average people and top people
in most companies.
The top people always do what is
expected...and then some.
They are thoughtful of others; they are
considerate and kind...and then some.
They meet their responsibilities fairly
and squarely...and then some.
They are good friends and helpful
neighbors...and then some.
They can be counted on in an
emergency...and then some.
I am thankful for people like this,
for they make the world a better place.
Their spirit of service is summed up
in these three little words...
and then some.

—Carl Holmes

9
GREAT SERVICE
BRINGS CUSTOMERS
BACK

9

Truly great service will bring customers back again and again. A friend of mine understood how a store creates loyal customers when he went to Nordstrom one day to get some perfume for his wife's birthday. The woman behind the counter said, "I'm sorry, we don't sell that perfume in our store. But I know where I can get it in the mall. How long are you going to be in our store?"

"About thirty minutes," he said.

"Fine, I'll go get it, bring it back, gift wrap it, and have it ready for you when you leave." This woman literally left Nordstrom, went to another store, got the perfume he wanted, came back to Nordstrom, and gift wrapped it. You know what she charged him? The same price she had paid at the other store. So Nordstrom didn't make any money on the deal, but what did they make? A lifelong customer—a raving fan.

The woman who grabbed Johnny's manager's hand to tell him, "Now I come in every time I go by…" highlights the impact great service has on bringing customers back.

"He profits most who serves best."

—Arthur F. Sheldon

10
THE FINAL TRUTH: GREAT SERVICE COMES FROM THE HEART

By Barbara Glanz

10

I wholeheartedly agree with Ken's Simple Truths of Great Service but would like to add one more:

Great Service Comes from the Heart.

Great customer service has to come from the inside out. You cannot mandate it. You can't threaten, reward, or coerce people to care. You can only awaken the desire and then give them the permission and encouragement to make it come alive in their work.

Simply said, if people don't have the desire in their hearts to serve and make a difference for others, they will not give great service. Mary Kay Ash, the founder of Mary Kay Cosmetics, often said the secret of her success was hiring nice people and then allowing them to be as nice as they could be.

Johnny's idea wasn't nearly as innovative as it was loving. During my speech, I challenged him to go home and think about something he could do to make his customers feel special. He thought about that idea and framed it in a way he could understand. He didn't bother reading management books or looking for the trend of the month; he searched inside himself for a solution. What he found—his Thought for the Day—was real. And it came from his heart, and that's the part you can't pretend.

At the core of great customer service lies the heart of each employee. When I work with an organization, I often walk around and ask people, "What is your work?" What they almost always tell me is a job description or a job title. Yet we are all so much more than that. We can bring our hearts to work with us! When you think about the question—"What is your work?"— think about this:

How is what you do every day making someone's life better? That is your very important work!

Johnny brought his heart to his job. He focused on what he could do in his daily work to make his customers feel special and their lives a little better.

No matter what our job or position may be, we each possess a unique understanding of this world and have our own ideas and gifts to share. Our truest gifts, like the one Johnny shared, can be found in our hearts if we look deeply enough and listen closely. When the heart is in the right place, the ego gets out of the way. That's when great service comes shining through.

THE FINAL TRUTH
IS THIS:

Great service comes from the heart.

The inspiration Johnny provided didn't stop in the store. When I shared the story with my musician friend David Roth, he was inspired to write the following song.

A Little Something More*

I run a local grocery store,
a friendly place to shop.
One day a boy came to my
market looking for a job.
He said his name was Johnny,
I could see that he was different.
I also saw a sparkle in his eye,
and so I hired him.

I started him collecting carts
and sweeping up the floor.
In no time flat, young Johnny
was a bagger in my store.
He took such pride and worked
so hard it rubbed off on my crew.
And just because he only did
the best that he could do.

Johnny is a bagger in
our local grocery store,
packing people's food away as
they go out the automatic door.
Just a job ten thousand
other people do;
but Johnny found a way
to make it new.

Johnny came to work one
Monday grinning ear to ear.
He told me that his dad was teaching
him to use the home computer.
Typing this and printing that,
whatever he had done.
The look on Johnny's face
that day was brighter than
the Indiana summer sun.

A couple weeks went by and
I began to notice something.

It started in the parking lot after people
had done their shopping.
They were digging through their
groceries and coming out with smiles.
I made a mental note and came inside
to check the aisles.

The store was pretty busy,
must be five o'clock, I guessed.
And here the line in Johnny's lane
was twice as long as all the rest.
"No waiting on one through four,"
I said, they didn't seem to care.
"We want to be in Johnny's line,"
they said, and stayed right there.

That's when I discovered
Johnny's magic secret brainstorm.
A little note he put in every shopper's
bag before they went home.

And every note had what he called
his "thought" for that same day.
And Johnny signed the back of
each good thought he gave away.

I can't begin to tell you how
the mood in our store shifted.
Whoever heard of coming home
from shopping so uplifted?
We see new people every day
we've never seen before.
And some folks say they come in
now each time they pass our store.

Of course Johnny's got the
longest lines of any shop in town.
He's also got some syndrome
that the doctors label "Down".
If you ask me how one person
makes a difference anymore,
come on by, see Johnny at our store.

Johnny is a bagger in

our local grocery store,

packing people's food away

as they go out the automatic door.

And he's making things a little

better than they were before.

The most important

person in our store,

Johnny always gives

a little something more.

I run a local grocery store,

a friendly place to shop.

One day a boy came to

my market looking for a job…

ABOUT THE AUTHORS

KEN BLANCHARD

Ken Blanchard is one of the most influential leadership experts in the world. He is the coauthor of sixty-five bestselling books, including the iconic bestseller *The New One Minute Manager®*, perennial favorite *Raving Fans*, and his latest, *Servant Leadership in Action*. His books have combined sales of more than twenty-one million copies in forty-two languages. In 2005, Ken was inducted into Amazon's Hall of Fame as one of the top twenty-five bestselling authors of all time.

Ken and his wife, Margie, are cofounders of The Ken

Blanchard Companies® (kenblanchard.com), a leading international training and consulting firm. In addition to being a renowned speaker and consultant, Ken is also cofounder of Lead Like Jesus, a global ministry dedicated to helping people become servant leaders.

Find out more about Ken and his books at kenblanchardbooks.com, and follow him on Twitter at @kenblanchard and on Facebook at facebook.com/KenBlanchardFanPage.

"Profit is the applause you get for taking care of your customers and creating a motivating environment for your people."

—Ken Blanchard

BARBARA GLANZ

Barbara Glanz, CSP, CPAE, is a member of the prestigious Speaker Hall of Fame and works with organizations that want to improve morale, retention, and service, as well as with people who want to rediscover the joy in their work and in their lives.

She is the first speaker on record to have spoken on all seven continents and in all fifty states to organizations as diverse as Nordstrom, Honda, Southwest Airlines, Bank of America, IBM, Kaiser Permanente, Hallmark, the U.S. Department of Energy, Hilton Hotels, Publix Supermarkets, Disney, the State of Michigan, Chick-fil-A, and the Singapore Security Police.

Meetings & Conventions magazine voted her "Best Keynote Presenter You Have Heard or Used," and she was recently selected as a "Legend of the Speaking Profession." She has been one of the top speakers at the Society for Human Resource Management's international convention since 1997.

Barbara is the author of twelve books, including *The Simple Truths of Appreciation*, *180 Ways to Spread Contagious Enthusiasm*, *CARE Packages for the Workplace*, *CARE Packages for the Home*, and *CARE Packages for your Customers*.

Known as the business speaker who speaks to your heart as well as to your head, she lives and breathes her personal motto, "Spreading Contagious Enthusiasm.™" She lives on the beach in Sarasota, Florida, and adores her four grandchildren, Gavin, Kinsey, Owen, and Simon. She can be reached at barbaraglanz.com or bglanz@barbaraglanz.com.

In every interaction
you have a **CHOICE**
to create a minus (-),
a zero (0), or a plus
(+) for that customer.
Always aim to
create a plus.

—Barbara A. Glanz